D1826277

9780853611011

Locomotion Papers

THE
NIDD VALLEY
RAILWAY

D. J. CROFT

THE OAKWOOD PRESS

1972

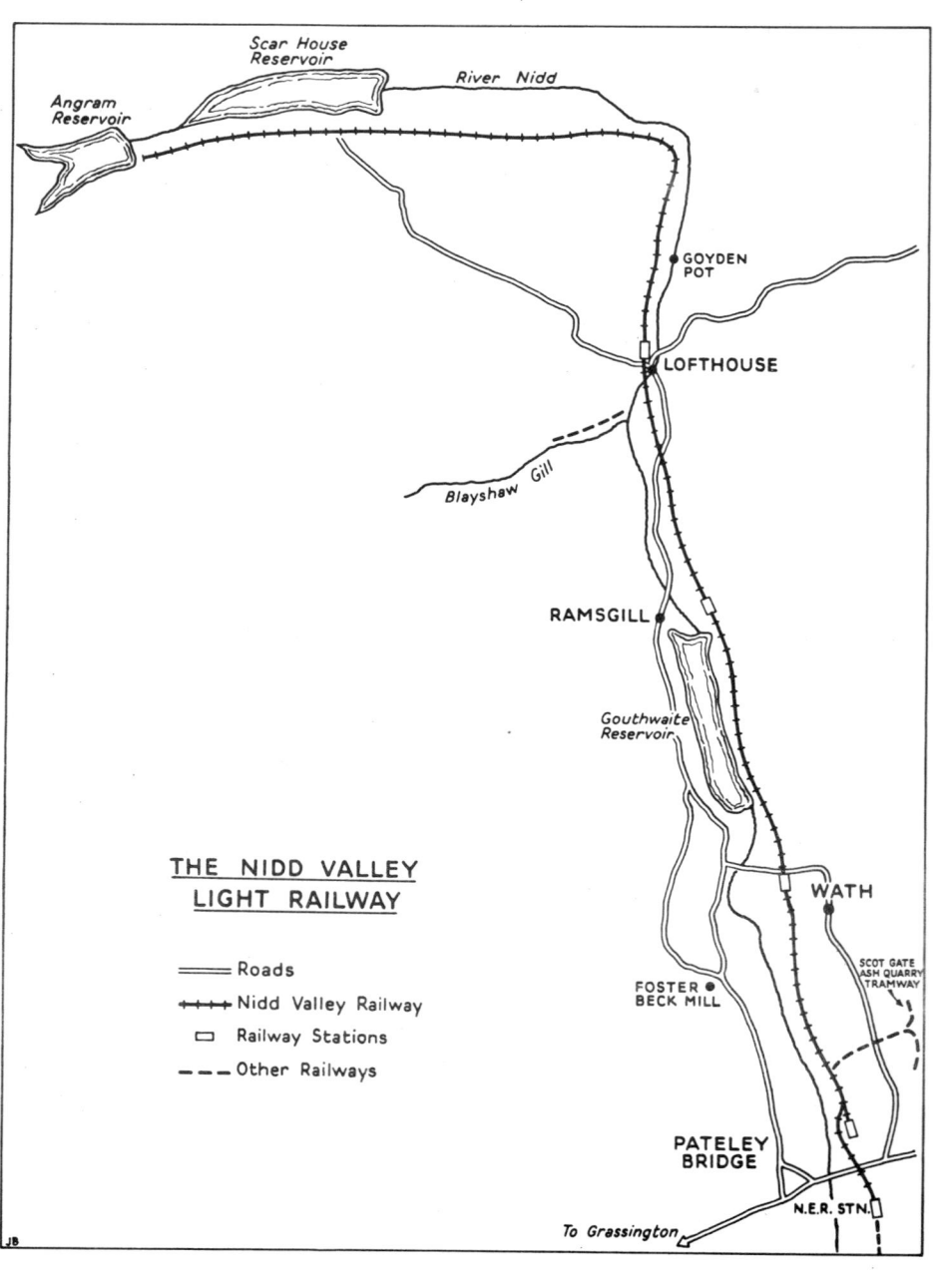

Scar House
Reservoir

River Nidd

Angram
Reservoir

● GOYDEN
POT

☐ LOFTHOUSE

Blayshaw Gill

RAMSGILL ●   ☐

Gouthwaite
Reservoir

☐   WATH ●

SCOT GATE
ASH QUARRY
TRAMWAY

FOSTER ●
BECK MILL

THE NIDD VALLEY
LIGHT RAILWAY

═══ Roads
╈╈╈╈ Nidd Valley Railway
☐ Railway Stations
─ ─ ─ Other Railways

PATELEY
BRIDGE

N.E.R. STN. ☐

To Grassington

JB

INTRODUCTION

The valley of the River Nidd, in the West Riding of Yorkshire, is nearly 55 miles long, beginning at Great Whernside, and ending at Nun Monkton where the Nidd flows into the River Ouse. However, the area known as Nidderdale extends for only about a half of the length, and forms a compact geographical region of its own. Despite this length, and great scenic beauty, it remains to this day one of the forgotten valleys of the Yorkshire Dales.

The area of Nidderdale can be divided into roughly two equal sections, with the market town of Pateley Bridge between the two. The first substantial historical accounts of Nidderdale appeared in Domesday Book of 1086. However, some of the local lead mines were worked in the time of the Brigantes, whilst several surrounding localities suggest Roman occupation.

Nidderdale has several industries, notably quarrying and lead mining, and a small textile industry. There is also a small slate quarry, a marble quarry, and a long, thin ironstone vein stretching along the valley. Throughout the ages, however, Nidderdale has had prosperity alternating with decline. As the early mining industry began to decline, so textiles became important around the thirteenth century. This too tended to decline by the seventeenth century, and mining became important once more. Unfortunately, the prosperity of the lead mining era passed, and so too did the prosperity of Nidderdale.

This period of decline lasted until 1862, when the North Eastern Railway opened its line from Harrogate to Pateley Bridge, thus opening this remote valley to the outside world. Prior to this, the only roads out of the dale had been to Grassington, Ripon and Kirkby Malzeard, and the only regular connection with the outside world had been the Nidderdale Omnibus, a double-deck horse bus, linking Pateley Bridge with trains of the Leeds & Thirsk Railway at Ripley. This operated from August 1st, 1849, until the opening of the railway, and ran twice daily.

With the opening of the railway, decline set in again. And so the years passed, and it seemed that the decline would continue endlessly, though the twentieth century was just around the corner, and for the next thirty years or so, the dale was to see much activity, in yet another spell of prosperity.

Yet for all this lengthy valley, our story is concerned with a mere thirteen or so miles between Pately Bridge and the head of the valley, for it is in these parts that the Nidd Valley Light Railway was conceived, constructed and closed. All this happened within a period of less than forty years.

Early Beginnings:

The origins of the Nidd Valley Light Railway, the first municipal passenger railway to be opened in Great Britain, can be traced back to the year 1901, when the Light Railway Commissioners granted the construction of a narrow gauge railway from Pateley Bridge to Lofthouse, a distance of six miles. This was the culmination of several years of work by local quarry owner John Metcalfe, and several local landowners, to establish a railway link between Pateley Bridge and the villages at the head of the Nidd Valley.

Before continuing the development of this line, it is necessary to examine earlier attempts to construct railways in the valley, as the N.V.L.R. was to stem from these early developments.

Several schemes had been initiated to construct a railway from Pateley Bridge down the Nidd Valley to Harrogate, and it was Metcalfe's plan to construct a line from the upper area of the Nidd Valley to meet this line at Pateley Bridge. The first survey of the area was made in 1818 by Messrs. Telford and Palmer, to construct a single line railway, with passing places, between Knaresborough and Pateley Bridge at a cost of £38,830.

Nothing came of this survey, and it was 1849 before anything else was done to provide efficient communications for this isolated valley. In that year, the Leeds & Thirsk Railway Company surveyed a route, and obtained powers to construct a railway between Starbeck (on the main line of the Leeds & Thirsk Co.), and Pateley Bridge. However, these powers lapsed.

Meanwhile, the North Eastern Railway were attempting to project lines into an area which it considered it should serve, with the aim of providing the town of Harrogate with better communications. Consequently, the North Eastern Railway obtained powers in 1859 to construct and operate a line from Nidd Bridge Junction to Pateley Bridge, and as we shall see later, this line was opened to traffic on May 1st, 1862.

Some years later, it became apparent that a railway was needed in the upper part of the dale. In the meantime, the Nidd Valley branch of the N.E.R. had been constructed and opened, and it was obvious from this line's success, that a similar line from Pateley Bridge to the head of the valley would be most advantageous.

As mentioned earlier, John Metcalfe and the other local landowners succeeded in getting the Light Railway Commissioners to give sanction for the construction of a line, a 2'6" gauge line, from Pateley Bridge to Lofthouse, the order being dated March 30th, 1901.

History at this point seems a little confused. It seems evident that Metcalfe and the others were not the actual owners of the Light Railway Order, but merely acting on behalf of the owners. This is supported by the fact that in May 1900 a syndicate entitled 'Power & Traction Limited' of Bridge Street, Westminster, successfully applied to construct a light railway of 2'6" gauge from Pateley Bridge to Lofthouse. This company had other local interests at the time as they owned the Ripon & District Light Railway, which had been authorised as a 3'6" gauge electric tramway from the City of Ripon to Studley Royal, a distance of 3½ miles. This line, however, was never built, neither was another line planned in the area. This was the Kirkby Malzeard Light Railway Company, authorised in 1907 for a six mile electric tramway to Ripon. If these two lines had been built, it might have been possible for extensions to have been constructed to connect with the Nidd Valley Light Railway at Pateley Bridge.

Prospects at this time seemed good as Bradford Corporation was at that time engaged on the construction of reservoirs in the Nidd Valley, a project which had begun in 1893 with the building of Gouthwaite Reservoir and which was to continue until 1929.

However, all was not well. Metcalfe and the others were unable to raise the required capital, and the order for the line was left to lapse shortly after it was issued.

Nothing further was done until 1904, when Bradford Corporation took over the powers to construct the line in conjunction with the building of their reservoirs in the valley. The Bradford Corporation (Nidd Valley) Transfer, Light Railway Order, 1904, was drawn up and the powers for the line were duly handed over to the Corporation.

Meanwhile, at a meeting of the Bradford Corporation Waterworks Committee on December 8th, 1903, a resolution was passed that authority be obtained to change the gauge of the line from 2'6" to 3'0".

Construction Begins:

By 1904 construction of Bradford's reservoirs in the Nidd Valley was well under way. Gouthwaite Reservoir, which was the first to be constructed, was begun in September 1893 and completed in 1901. The reservoir was designed not to increase the water supply to Bradford, but to provide water power for local industry.

So, by 1904, the Corporation was ready to begin its larger projects in the valley.

Having obtained powers for the line, Bradford Corporation made a start on construction, first borrowing £30,000, a sum which it was hoped would suffice for the entire construction, but which later turned out to be a serious miscalculation.

It was decided to construct the line to standard gauge instead of 3'0" to enable transhipment of materials from the North Eastern Railway at Pateley Bridge. The Corporation had originally planned to use the line solely for the construction of their reservoirs, but they were obliged to provide a passenger service to meet the Board of Trade requirements and so, finally, the dreams of John Metcalfe had been realised.

The cutting of the first sod took place on July 13th, 1904, when Alderman Holdsworth, the Chairman of the railway, began the work of construction near the head of Gouthwaite Reservoir.

The line was laid with rail of 56 lbs. per yard, and was of the flat-bottomed type. The entire line was single track and there were many sharp curves, the minimum being nine chains, and also several steep gradients, the maximum being 1 in 50.

In all, a line of 12½ miles was constructed between Pateley Bridge and Angram, the site of the Corporation's next reservoir. It had originally been intended that the line should only be 6 miles in length, and indeed, this is as far as the line was operated for passenger traffic, the remaining 6½ miles being used solely for the carriage of materials and supplies.

Work on the line progressed according to plan, almost until the completion of the line, when the opening was delayed from the summer of 1906 until September 11th, 1907.

The question now arose of purchasing rolling stock for the line. To begin operations, two 4–4–0 tank locomotives were purchased from the Metropolitan Railway. These locos were from two different classes, No.20, built in 1866, and No.34, built in 1879, both by Beyer, Peacock. They were numbered 1 and 2 by the Nidd Valley Light Railway, and were given the names 'Holdsworth' and 'Milner'. These names originated, along with those of many other locomotives the line was to own, from people connected with the line. 'Holdsworth' was named after Alderman Holdsworth, who had cut the first sod of the line in 1904, whilst 'Milner' was named after a Conservative Alderman on Bradford City Council.

The reason for the purchase of these locos was that they had been specially built for the Metropolitan to negotiate sharp curves, and were thus ideally suited to the N.V.L.R., having been replaced on their old duties on Underground services by electric trains.

When they were purchased by the Nidd Valley, both engines had the condensing apparatus removed, and they were altered and repainted at Neasden before delivery to Pateley Bridge.

Coaching stock was required too, and so, tenders were put out for two first and third class composite carriages, and three third class carriages. However, the Corporation decided not to continue the tender, and instead, purchased ten four-wheeled coaches from the Metropolitan Railway at £80 each and these were repainted and refurbished at a total cost of £463.11.6. The engines were painted maroon with gold lining, with both the Bradford Corporation coat of arms, and 'The Nidd Valley Light Railway'. The coaches were similarly treated.

All the goods stock for the line was purchased new and was painted grey, with 'BC' in large white letters.

One other vehicle was purchased for the opening of the line, this being the Bradford Corporation Tramways 'Private Car'. This was a saloon vehicle, similar to a tram in appearance, and was in fact built by Hurst, Nelson, and had been ordered in February 1904.

And so, after a little more than three years, the line was ready to be opened, and to become the first municipally owned light railway in Britain.

At the Board of Trade Inspection, Colonel Van Donop stated that ... "the line appears to be in all respects very soundly constructed, and the station buildings are exceptionally good for a line of this description. The signalling arrangements are considerably in excess of the Board of Trade requirements for light railways."

The Line in Operation:

The line was opened to traffic on September 11th, 1907, by the Lord Mayor of Bradford, Alderman J.A.Godwin, though the passenger service did not begin until the following day. This was the first occasion for a Lord Mayor to drive a railway locomotive. The line also had the added distinction of being the first municipally-owned railway to carry passengers.

For the opening ceremony, a special train was used to carry the civic party, and this consisted of locomotive 'Holdsworth', acquired from the Metropolitan Railway, the Bradford Corporation Tramways Private Car, and three carriages. This train travelled as far as Lofthouse, where a contractor's locomotive took over from 'Holdsworth' to haul the train for the remainder of the journey to Scar House.

At Scar House, a lunch was served for the party in the Reading Room. Alderman Holdsworth, the Chairman of the line, was to have presided at the celebrations but illness prevented him taking the chair, though he was able to attend. Alderman Milner was also absent due to illness. This is somewhat ironical as the first two locomotives on the line were named after these officials! As a result, Mr. William Land, the Deputy Lord Mayor presided.

The Chairman, Alderman Holdsworth, presented the Lord Mayor with an 18 carat gold medallion as a token of their esteem. This medallion contained a design with locomotive 'Holdsworth' in the centre, with the city motto 'Labor Omnia Vincit' at the base of the medallion. The Lord Mayor followed by saying that it was not every municipality that would have the pluck to tackle an undertaking like the building of the railway, and he wished every success to the undertaking.

Mr. T.Snowden was entrusted with the task of replying to this toast, and said that all felt proud to think that the Bradford Corporation railway was successfully inaugurated. He gave the Lord Mayor credit for his skilful driving of the engine from Pateley to the end of the line, and expressed a fervent hope that he would take them back as safely!

The guest list at this event was quite impressive, including most of the City Council, local landowners, and representatives of both the North Eastern Railway and, surprisingly, the Midland Railway.

Strictly speaking, the railway was worked in two separate sections, Pateley Bridge to Lofthouse, by the Nidd Valley Light Railway, and the Lofthouse to Angram section, which was worked by the contractors. A certain amount of through running did take place, however. Two contractor's locomotives were regularly used on through trains of cement and coal from Pateley Bridge to Scar in later years, these being 0—6—0 tank locomotives 'Gadie' and 'Blythe'. When extra workers trains were needed 'Milner' was usually used, whilst the lighter locos were used on the dam and round the reservoir and quarry.

Through running did not always take place. Each day a goods train arrived at Pateley Bridge (N.V.) from the London & North Eastern Railway, carrying supplies for the Angram site. A Nidd Valley loco hauled the train as far as Lofthouse in the morning, and in the afternoon a contractor's locomotive would come down from Angram to haul the five-van train up to the site. This engine was usually an 0—6—0 tank engine.

As mentioned in the previous section, it had been estimated that £30,000 would suffice for the construction and equipment of the line, but by May 1908 it was evident that this figure was insufficient, and so, an application was made to the Light Railway Commissioners by Bradford Corporation for an order to increase the amount, and by the time the line was fully equipped, a further £32,726 had been sanctioned. The order read as follows:—

"**Bradford Corporation (Nidd Valley) Light Railway Orders, (Amendment) Order, 1908.**

Order Amending the Bradford Corporation (Nidd Valley) Transfer, Light Railway Order, 1904.

Whereas by the Nidd Valley Light Railway Order, 1901, (hereinafter called 'the Order of 1901'), the Nidd Valley Light Railway Company were authorised to make and maintain the Light Railway, (hereinafter called 'the railway'), therein described, from Pateley Bridge to Lofthouse in the West Riding of the County of York.

And whereas, by the Bradford Corporation (Nidd Valley Transfer) Light Railway Order, (hereinafter called 'The Order of 1904'), the power of the said Company with reference to the construction and working of the railway, and otherwise incidental thereto, were transferred to the Lord Mayor, Aldermen and citizens of the City of

Bradford, (hereinafter called 'the Corporation').

And whereas by the Order of 1904, the Corporation were authorised to borrow for the purposes referred to in that order such sums as might be required, not exceeding 30,000 pounds.

And whereas, the Corporation have proceeded in exercise of the powers conferred upon them by the said orders, with the construction and equipment of the railway.

And whereas, the said sum of £30,000 has been found insufficient to meet the expenditure involved in such construction and equipment. And whereas an application was in May 1908, duly made to the Light Railway Commissioners by the Corporation in pursuance of the Light Railways Act of 1896, for an order to increase the amount, which by the Order of 1904, the Corporation are authorised to borrow and to extend the period prescribed by the Order of 1904, within which the Corporation shall pay off moneys borrowed by them under the powers of that Order, as amended by this Order, and for other purposes."

The total cost of the line was somewhere in the region of £55,000, being divided as follows: —

1	Cost of Order and Transfer	£ 2,338
2	Land	£ 8,149
3	Railway	£28,630
4	Telephones, Electric Tablet, Signalling, etc.	£ 2,277
5	Station buildings	£ 2,850
6	Goods and car sheds	£ 1,144
7	Loco. shed	£ 189
8	Approach roads	£ 670
9	Rolling stock	£ 3,926
10	Printing, stationery	£ 1,421
11	Engineers, Inspectors, Clerk of Works	£ 2,609

£54,203

Two books published around the time of the opening of the railway have brief mention of the line; of Pateley Bridge, one states:

"With the opening this year of the railway 'up dale' to the romantic region of Middlesmoor, it seems likely that Pateley Bridge will become a great centre of attraction to visitors in the summer season.",

whilst the other had this to say of Lofthouse:

"While the calm and seclusion of the district around Lofthouse and Middlesmoor will be somewhat broken by the intrusion of the Light Railway in its midst, the facilities of transit will certainly be greatly enhanced."

Both of these statements were to prove true, for during the next twenty-five years or so, this part of Nidderdale was to see the biggest boom it had ever seen, or is likely to see.

In 1909, locomotive 'Milner' was sold, and replaced by a new loco bearing the same name. This was bought from Hudswell, Clarke and was an 0—6—0 tank engine.

By 1910, the line was paying its way, as the following figures show. Expenditure amounted to £2,044 whilst receipts totalled £4,137, a total profit of £2,093. Figures for passengers and goods carried on the line in 1910 are also encouraging, 45,344 passengers and 13,167 tons of freight travelled over the line in this year.

During the next few years, the line was to continue its profitable course, for by 1916, more plans were being prepared by the Corporation for further reservoirs in the valley, which, in turn, would result in greater prosperity for the line.

Only one thing seemed likely to impede the prosperity of the line. This had been the outbreak of war in 1914 when Angram Reservoir was almost complete, many men had left the site to join the war and this severely hampered the work. The Local Government Board insisted that all work on the project should cease until the end of hostilities, but Bradford needed water, as was evident to the Fire Brigade, and so, deputations were sent to London and the work was allowed to continue, though the Nidd Aqueduct scheme was held up by the war in 1917.

Even during these stringent times, however, plans were being prepared for Scar House Reservoir, and so, once again, the prosperity of the railway was assured.

Shortly after the war, locomotive 'Holdsworth' was scrapped at Scar House, thus reducing the locomotive stock to one, excluding the contractor's locomotives.

1919 saw the completion of the Angram Reservoir scheme, but on October 5th, 1921, there began another period of activity for the line, with the cutting of the first sod of Scar House Reservoir.

1921 was also an important one for the line, because in this year its most unusual item of motive power was purchased, a steam railcar.

The railcar concerned had been built in October 1905 for the Great Western Railway by Kerr, Stuart as number 15. Only two of this type were purchased, and bodies fitted at Swindon, although other types of railcar were to become a notable feature of Great Western operation. It was sold by them in May 1920 to a Mr. J.F.Wake, but was re-sold in 1921 to the N.V.L.R. The car was 50'0½" in length and seated 48 passengers. The mechanical portion was arranged so that, with the boiler (arranged transversely), engine tank, etc., all located at one end, it was possible for the railcar to be driven from either end. It also contained luggage space, and was fitted with vacuum brakes and a steam brake. It was painted maroon, with the railway's name and the Bradford Corporation crest on both sides, and bore the name 'Hill', after the Lord Mayor of Bradford in 1908–1909.

It has been said that statistics can be made to prove almost anything, but the figures for the Nidd Valley Light Railway, which are available for the years 1923 and 1925, are proof in themselves of the success of the railway. Expenditure on the line amounted to £2,999 in 1923, with receipts totalling £7,112, making a total profit of £4,113. Traffic had also increased greatly on the line, with 59,790 passengers travelling on the line in 1925, and 26,222 tons of freight, almost twice as much as in 1910.

At about this time, twelve four-wheeled coaches were purchased from the Maryport & Carlisle Railway, which had just recently been merged, under the 1923 grouping of the railways. These were used mainly to replace those purchased from the Metropolitan Railway on the opening of the line, back in 1907, and the rolling stock figures for 1927 showed that the stock consisted of these 12 vehicles, plus two Metropolitan coaches and 1 private saloon. Goods stock at that time totalled 8 vehicles.

1929 was the year when the decline of the railway set in. On April 12th it was decided to close the line, and immediately the North Eastern Railway were approached to see whether they would be interested in taking over the line and stock, but they replied that it would not be in the interests of the company.

As a result, the passenger service ended on December 31st, 1929.

During the last nine months of operation, 24,906 passengers had been carried.

From now on, the line was concerned solely with the carriage of supplies to the reservoir site at Scar House, and in 1929 this work was at its peak with over 700 men being employed on the site.

For the next four years or so work progressed on the Scar House project and by 1934 the work was nearly completed, but a drought during the summer of that year caused the reservoir to be put into use before completion. However, the reservoir was not finally completed until September 7th, 1936, when Alderman Sir Anthony Gadie put the last stone in place at Scar House Dam.

This completed Bradford Corporation's vast reservoir plan, which had begun back in 1893 with the building of Gouthwaite Reservoir, and together the three reservoirs Gouthwaite, Angram and Scar House had cost a total of £2,764,675, which was far in excess of the 1932 estimated total of £1,300,000.

With all work on the site finished, there was now little reason for the Corporation to maintain the Nidd Valley Light Railway, and with the added competition from bus services operated by the West Yorkshire Road Car Co. in the area, which at that time included a service from Pateley Bridge to

Scar, on Saturdays only, as well as a Harrogate—Pateley Bridge—Lofthouse service, the last schedule train travelled over the N.V.L.R. late in 1936, so bringing to an end an era of prosperity for Upper Nidderdale, which had lasted only three decades.

The Contractor's Line:

As mentioned previously, the section of the line from Lofthouse to Angram was worked by the contractors, and in practice was typical of many other industrial railways, though this stretch of the line had many outstanding qualities which caused it to be referred to in an article in the 'Railway Magazine' for 1927, as "probably one of the most interesting railway routes in the British Isles".

Above Lofthouse, the terminus of passenger services on the Nidd Valley Light Railway, the gradient rises to 1 in 40, with many sharp curves, the minimum being 9 chains. Half way to Scar House was a tunnel, 180 yds. in length cut through solid limestone, though there was an avoiding line around the tunnel. Also on this section, the track was not fenced off, and there were no mileposts and no gradient indicators. Because of the gradients and the severity of the line in general, numerous water-towers and coaling stations were situated between Lofthouse and Angram, which were frequently used by through trains of supplies and materials to the reservoir sites.

The Scar House reservoir site was probably the most distinguishing feature on the whole Nidd Valley Line, for it was here that the contractors built an entire village for the workmen engaged upon the site. At this remote outpost, nearly 1250 feet above sea level, lived in 1929 (when work on the Scar House project was in full swing) over 700 men, in a village consisting of 10 hostels and 62 bungalows. Besides these, was a hospital, bakery, school, laundry, stores, Post Office, concert hall, cinema, reading room, recreation room, canteen, church and resident doctor. Electric light was used in all these, supplied by hydro-electric power from Angram Reservoir.

It seems apparent from various sources that the track layout at Scar House varied as time went on. At the height of construction at Scar House, the site had a single track leaving the main line, with sidings from this in various directions. At least one source indicates that tracks extended across the River Nidd by means of a small bridge, and this fact is substantiated by an aerial view of the site taken about 1965, which clearly shows the earthworks and layout of the tracks. It seems that on completion of the Scar House project, merely one siding was left there, the remainder of the track being removed, probably to Angram on commencement of that project.

Scar House Reservoir itself has one of the biggest dams in Europe, the wall being 1800 feet long with a maximum height of 170 feet. It covers an area of 180 acres and is 154 feet deep, and during its construction 13 locomotives were in use, along with 25 locomotive cranes and 3 steam navvies. The stone for the construction was obtained from the hills above the site, and was transported down to the site on an incline, at the foot of which was a stone dressing plant and a stone crushing plant, which reduced the stone to six inch cubes.

The whole work at Scar House took 15 years, the first 3½ years being taken up with excavating the site, during which time 460,000 cubic yards of earth was removed. The reservoir was opened on September 7th, 1936, by Alderman Sir Anthony Gadie, who had also laid the first concrete in place at the site on June 17th, 1924.

A little less than two miles beyond Scar House Dam lies Angram Reservoir, at the very head of the valley. Work had begun on this reservoir before the Nidd Valley Light Railway had been built, the first sod having been cut on August 13th, 1904. Work on this site also took 15 years, despite the fact that the capacity of Angram is only half that of Scar House, the war having caused great delays in the work. During the construction, Angram was the base of the contractors operations, and the site included a locomotive shed, carriage shed, workshops, offices, coaling stages and weighing machines. The bed of the reservoir is solid limestone, which was discovered during the excavations. This reservoir is a mile long and ⅓ mile wide and was completed in 1919.

After the completion of the Angram Reservoir, the track was removed as far as Scar House, ready for the commencement of that project in 1921.

A feat of engineering as large as the reservoirs project could not have been accomplished without the use of many locomotives and, at one time, as many as 13 were employed on the Scar House site. The engines used on this section of the N.V.L.R. were mostly on hire, many of them being new, though some had been transferred from other railways. In general, the lighter locos were used on the dam and around the reservoir and quarry, whilst the heavier ones were used on trains of materials from Pateley Bridge to the sites. Details of the engines used will be found in a subsequent chapter.

After the Last Train:

When the last train had run to Scar House, late in 1936, the next task to be undertaken was the dismantling of the line and the disposal of its equipment. The first sections of track were lifted early in 1937, and sold to Messrs. Maden & McKee, Ltd., of Liverpool, in February of that year. The final blow, however, came on June 16th, 1937, when an auction was held to dispose of the rest of the railway, so great was the amount to be sold that the auction was not completed until June 19th. The following items were sold:—

Eight locomotives, aged between 12 and 46 years old, some four-wheeled coaches, goods stock, 14 miles of track, signalling, the entire Scar Village, and some of the contractor's plant. The 12½ acres of land between Pateley Bridge and Wath were bought by a private firm, whilst the Wath to Lofthouse section was purchased by the local council to build a road. The locomotives which did not find new owners were scrapped.

After the auction, when everything had been disposed of, seemingly for all time, one item from the railway was to re-appear over thirty years later. This was 'Hill', the steam railcar, which was found in a Leeds scrapyard a few years ago, still bearing G.W.R. notices and fittings, despite the fact that it had been sold for scrap in October 1937.

The very last train to run on the line was an un-scheduled one run by the contractors during the dismantling of the line, and with this, there came to an end the busiest and most prosperous era this part of Nidderdale had seen, or is likely to see.

To conclude the story of the Nidd Valley Light Railway, it would seem fitting to end with a passage from the 'Railway Magazine' for September 1937, which seems to describe exactly the atmosphere of Upper Nidderdale some thirty years ago:—

"When all this is cleared away, and the last train has gone clanking down the lonely valley, there will be little to show, besides the two towering dams, and the great tranquil lakes, what a hive of industry this bleak and desolate spot once was . . . . . .

"By the passing of the Nidd Valley Light Railway, the dwindling company of light railways in this country will be the poorer for the loss of one of its most interesting members . . . . ."

Description of the Line:

No historical account of the Nidd Valley Light Railway would be complete without a description of the line itself, together with its surroundings, from the busy market town of Pateley Bridge to the quiet area around Lofthouse, and the barren moorlands and valleys of Scar House and Angram.

The station in Pateley Bridge was a few minutes walk away from the foot of the main street, in the opposite direction to the N.E.R. station. On the wall of the station was a plaque which read:—

The opening day, September 11th, 1907, with the official party and train at Scar Village; official saloon and ex-Metropolitan coaches.

Locomotive 'Holdsworth' and the official party on the opening day. The Lord Mayor is on the footplate. Both Photos. Courtesy of Bradford City Water Department.

*Locomotive 'Gadie' and 'Illingworth' on a train to Scar House Reservoir.
Courtesy of Bradford City Water Department.*

The railcar 'Hill' at Pateley Bridge (Loco. Pub. Co.)

Close-up view of the unusual tipping wagons used on the reservoir construction work.

The elusive 'Illingworth' – no written details appear to survive about this locomotive!

Another mystery! Another 'Gadie'. It is likely that one of the 0–4–0's has had the nameplates from 'Gadie' transferred to it. The occasion for the Union Jack is also unknown.

Track of line near Ramsgill, 1971 (R. W. Kidner)

Lofthouse station in 1971 (R. W. Kidner)

"Nidd Valley Light Railway
opened by the
Rt.Hon., the Lord Mayor
Alderman Godwin, J.P.,
11th Sept. 1907
Mr. Alderman Holdworth, J.P., Chairman,
Mr. Alderman Milner, Dep. Chairman,
Frederick Stevens, Town Clerk,
John Best & Sons, Contractors,
John Watson, M.Inst.C.E.,
Wm. Thos. Croft, Secretary."

The station itself was quite large, with a booking-hall, two waiting rooms, and two platforms, though only one was usually used. There were several sidings, and a line which went beyond the station yard, to connect with the N.E.R. station some distance away. All passenger trains on the N.V.L.R. terminated at the line's own station, though goods trains did continue over to the other station to be turned. The station building itself was demolished in 1937, but unfortunately the plaque was lost without trace.

Soon after leaving Pateley Bridge, we pass the site of the former Scot Gate Ash Quarry Tramway. Now only the road bridge over the disused line is left, reminding us of this once active cable worked incline to the quarries on the hilltop. The line itself was in operation from about 1872 to 1892, when much of the tramway and the quarries were washed away during torrential storms, and after that date little work was done in the quarries, and by 1912 they were out of use. The incline was 600 feet long and in places the gradient was almost 1 in 3. The empty wagons were taken up the incline by the weight of the loaded ones coming down. Wagons could be stopped at any point, and at several places runaway sidings were laid to prevent disaster at the foot of the incline. The line had been built by Mr. George Metcalfe, one of the family concerned with the development of the Nidd Valley Light Railway at the turn of the century. 'Delphstone' was quarried at Scot Gate and provided stone for the National Gallery, the South Kensington Museums and the Albert Memorial in London.

Leaving Pateley Bridge behind, the railway paralleled the River Nidd for just over two miles before entering Wath Station. Half way between Pateley Bridge and Wath is Foster Beck Mill, with its large water-wheel 35 feet in diameter, which until a few years ago provided power for machinery to spin yarn from raw hemp. The adjoining premises have now been turned into a restaurant.

Wath Station consisted of a single through line, with two short sidings and a goods depot. All the station buildings on the line were alike in that they each had a booking office, waiting room, stores and a station master's house, though Wath had a more unusual history than the others. The building itself was originally a farmhouse but was converted into a hostel in 1895 for the use of Bradford Corporation workmen engaged on the Gouthwaite Reservoir project until 1901, when it was converted into the station for the opening of the line.

A little less than half a mile beyond Wath Station, Gouthwaite Reservoir begins and, for the next two miles, the railway ran right along the edge of the reservoir, until reaching the village of Ramsgill. The reservoir covers the site of Gouthwaite Hall, which had been built in the early seventeenth century, and at which the notorious schoolmaster-murderer, Eugene Aram, had taught for a time. Aram had in fact been born at Ramsgill in 1704. Instead of being pulled down, the Hall was left to sink below the waters of the reservoir when it was opened in 1901.

The station at Ramsgill was some distance from the village, and contained three short sidings and a long stock siding with a goods shed.

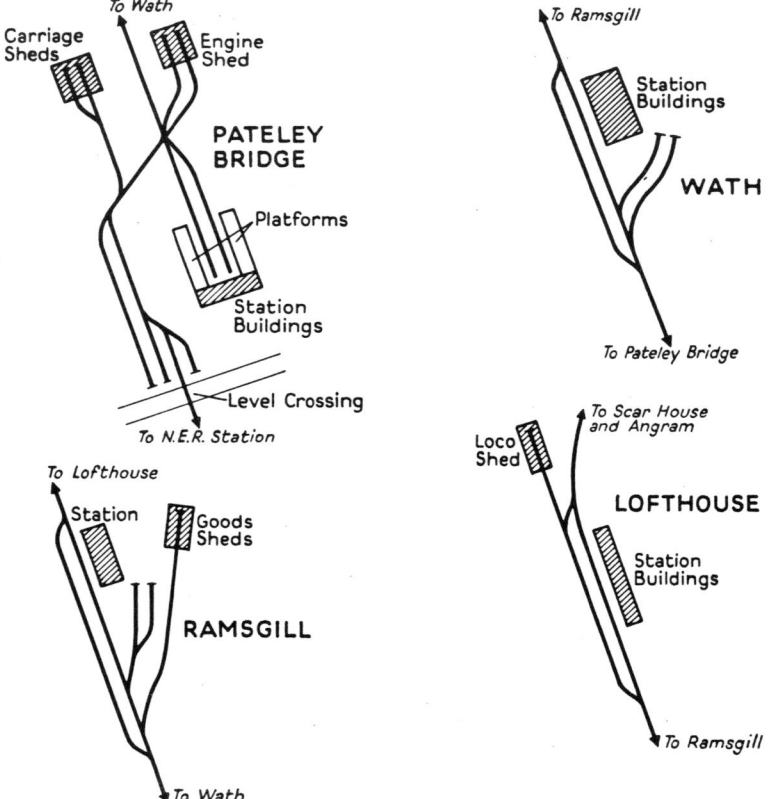

Continuing up the valley, the railway crossed the road near Low Sikes, and ran alongside the River Nidd until reaching Lofthouse Station, the terminus of passenger services. Lofthouse was a comparatively small station in comparison with others on the line, with only a single passing loop and a small shed, which had been built at a cost of £70 in 1907 to house the Bradford Corporation Tramways Private Car, but in later years was used as a small engine shed.

Beyond Lofthouse, the railway continued as the contractor's line and followed closely the contours of the valley. This section of the line passed several well-known scenic localities, such as Blayshaw Gill and Goyden Pot. Blayshaw Gill is an old lead working and on one occasion in 1905 was the scene of an unusual incident. A local resident, a Mr. J.Backhouse, went into the mine one Sunday and, during his return through the shaft, heard a truck on the narrow gauge mine tramway being pushed towards him, but there was nothing there. This occurrence had been experienced by others before him and was known locally as the Blayshaw Boggle.

Goyden Pot is a tunnel, two miles deep, running into the hillside, so dangerous is it that by 1932 only about 1200 yards had been explored.

And so we reach the reservoir sites of Scar House and Angram at the very head of the Nidd Valley, which for a time was Nidderdale's great railway centre. The village at Scar House, the awesome-looking steam-cranes and all the equipment that is used on such a vast undertaking as this, have all gone, and the area is just the same as it was at the turn of the century though, now, the vast reservoirs dominate the scene.

Gone, too, is the railway that served the inhabitants of these remote parts for only 29 years.

Looking back over the years, it seems a great pity that the line was not kept open, for a railway of this kind, in such a picturesque area, would have been a great attraction nowadays, not only to railway enthusiasts but to tourists who would have been able to see a thriving and unusual railway, equally of interest to the preserved railways of this country which are so well-known to tourists and enthusiasts alike.

ROLLING STOCK

Locomotives

The Nidd Valley Light Railway used four locomotives on its passenger service between Pateley Bridge and Lofthouse, the remaining engines being used by the contractors and were mainly on hire. Some had come from other railways, whilst others were bought new. The passenger locomotives were as follows: —

No.1. 'Holdsworth'   4—4—0T Beyer, Peacock, No.707, built 1866. Bought 1907 from Metropolitan Railway, No.20. Weight 45 tons, length 33'1". Condensing apparatus removed by Met. on purchase and altered and repainted at Neasden before delivery to N.V.L.R. This loco hauled the first train on the line and was named after Alderman Holdsworth who, as Chairman of the railway, had cut the first sod in construction of the line in 1904, and was also a member of Bradford City Council. Locomotive scrapped at Scar House about 1918/1919.

No.2. 'Milner'   4—4—0T Beyer, Peacock, No.1878, built 1879. Bought 1907 from Metropolitan Railway, No.34. Weight 46¾ tons, length 31'10". Condensing apparatus removed on purchase and altered and repainted at Neasden before delivery to N.V.L.R. Named after Alderman Milner, who was the Deputy Chairman of the railway. Sold 1909.

'Milner ' (II)   0—6—0T Hudswell, Clarke, No.882, built 1909. Fitted with a small, high speed reciprocating engine and dynamo for lighting the train, which were supplied by Harper, Phillips & Co.Ltd., of Grimsby. Assumed the name 'Milner' when the first loco was sold in 1909. Later sold to Sir Lindsay Parkinson, the contractor, and later to Caffin & Co., and George Wimpey.

'Hill'   Steam Railcar. Built 1905 for the Great Western Railway, No.15, by Kerr, Stuart, and supplied with engine number 0864. Sold to the Nidd Valley in 1921 via J.F.Wake. Contained luggage space and had seats for 48 passengers. Fitted with vacuum brakes and a steam brake. Sold for scrap June 1937, though found in a Leeds scrapyard nearly 30 years later.

Locomotives used by the contractors were as follows: —

'Blythe'   0—6—0T Avonside Engine Co., No.1894, built 1922. Used on through trains to the dams. Named after the Lord Mayor of Bradford, 1921.

'Gadie'   0—6—0T Barclay & Sons, No.1866, built 1925. Also used on through trains to the dams. Named after the Lord Mayor of Bradford who cut the first sod at Scar House on October 5th, 1921, and who also laid the first concrete on the site.

'Mitchell'   0—6—0T Hudswell, Clarke, No.1208, built 1916. Named after loco superintendent, Mr. C.Mitchell, appointed 1922.

'Watson'   0—6—0T Hudswell, Clarke, No.1197, built 1916. Named after earlier loco superintendent, Mr. James Watson.

'Craven'   0—4—0T Hudswell, Clarke, No.1411, built 1920. Sold to Gas Committee Nov. 1929, for £700.

'Haig'   0—6—0T Manning, Wardle, No.1224, built 1890. Named after Field Marshall Earl Haig of Bemersyde, who had been given the Freedom of the City of Bradford in 1921.

'Allenby'   0—6—0T Manning, Wardle, No.1379, built 1898.

'Beatty'   0—6—0T Manning, Wardle, No.1669, built 1905.

'Trotter'   0—4—0T Barclay & Sons, No.1810, built 1925. Named after Herbert M.Trotter, Lord Mayor of Bradford, 1924.

'Stringer'   0—4—0T Barclay & Sons, No.1877, built 1925. Named after the Lord Mayor of Bradford, 1925—1926.

'Kitchener'   0—6—0T Peckett, Sons, Ltd., No.939, built 1902.

'Ian Hamilton'   0—6—0T Hudswell, Clarke, No.480, built 1898.

There is also believed to have been an additional loco operated by the contractors, named 'Illingworth', but details of this are lacking.

Coaches

To commence the passenger service in 1907, ten four-wheeled coaches were purchased from the Metropolitan Railway. These vehicles were one class only and were operated as such until twelve further coaches were purchased from the Maryport & Carlisle Railway in the mid-1920's. By that time, only two of the ex-Met. coaches were still in use. As a result of these coaches arriving, two classes of travel were provided:—

1st — which was provided in the railcar, with the luxury of armrests and electric light, and

3rd and Workmen — both of these used the newly acquired coaches from and M. & C., and many of them still bore that railway's lettering.

One further vehicle must be mentioned. This was the Bradford Corporation Tramways Private Car. This saloon railway coach had been ordered from Hurst, Nelson in February 1904, and was used on the first train on the line. After this, it was only used for civic occasions and was returned to Hurst, Nelson after 1910, where its truck was used for another wagon or carriage, but the body remained there until about 1912, when it was acquired by the Wantage Tramway as their number 5.

At the auction in 1937, only several of the coaches remained to be sold, all others having been previously disposed of.

Goods Stock

Very few details of the goods stock have come to light. At the opening of the line, there were 8 goods vehicles, made up of two luggage/brake vans and six open goods wagons, all built by Hurst, Nelson.

Photographic evidence during the construction of Scar House Dam, reveals two types of goods vehicles in use. These were some very old side-tipping wagons, and several flat wagons which appear to have been used to carry concrete to the sites.

All remaining goods vehicles were sold during the 1937 auction.

Liveries

When the two Metropolitan locos were purchased, they retained the red livery of that railway but were lined out in yellow. Similarly, coaches were red, lined in yellow. In 1914, 0—6—0T 'Milner' was repainted black, with polished brass dome and copper topped chimney. By 1921, when 'Hill' was acquired, the livery had been changed to maroon, with maroon coaches. Some of the coaches carried the name 'Bradford Corporation', whilst others bore the initials 'N.V.L.R.', both with the coat of arms. Wagons were always grey with white lettering.

Timetables

To commence operations, four return trains were planned each day, and this timetable remained fairly rigid for several years. The following is the 1915 timetable:—

Pateley Bridge	8.40	10.20	1.30	4.10
Wath Station	8.45	10.25	1.35	4.15
Ramsgill	8.55	10.35	1.45	4.25
Lofthouse	9.00	10.40	1.50	4.30
Lofthouse	9.15	11.05	2.55	4.50
Ramsgill	9.20	11.10	3.00	4.55
Wath Station	9.30	11.20	3.10	5.05
Pateley Bridge	9.35	11.25	3.15	5.10

As the war progressed, it was found necessary to reduce the service to three trains daily, in each direction, as follows: —

Pateley Bridge	8.30	10.30	3.45
Wath Station	8.35	10.35	3.50
Ramsgill	8.48	10.48	4.03
Lofthouse	8.55	10.55	4.10
Lofthouse	9.15	12.00	4.20
Ramsgill	9.20	12.05	4.25
Wath Station	9.30	12.15	4.35
Pateley Bridge	9.35	12.20	4.40

This was the 1918 timetable and provided no trains on Sundays. Special services were operated on Bank Holidays, etc., as below: —

Boxing Day	— full service operated.
Christmas Eve, Easter Sat-) urday and Easter Monday)	— one train leaving Pateley Bridge at 5.00 p.m. to Lofthouse, returning from there at 5.30 p.m.
Christmas Day and) Good Friday)	— no trains

By 1922, when traffic was greater, a further return trip was added to the pre-war timetable, with slight alterations to timings, compared with the 1915 timetable, as shown below: —

Pateley Bridge	8.30	10.20	1.30	3.30	5.00
Wath Station	8.35	10.25	1.35	3.35	5.05
Ramsgill	8.47	10.37	1.47	3.47	5.17
Lofthouse	8.53	10.43	1.53	3.53	5.23
Lofthouse	9.10	11.00	2.00	4.10	5.30
Ramsgill	9.16	11.06	2.06	4.16	5.36
Wath Station	9.25	11.15	2.15	4.25	5.45
Pateley Bridge	9.30	11.20	2.20	4.30	5.50

In addition, various workmen's trains were operated, as this 1927 timetable shows: —

Scar Village	dep.	8.30	8.30	1.40
Lofthouse	arr.	9.30	9.30	2.20
Lofthouse	dep.	1.30	5.00	4.45
Scar Village	arr.	2.30	5.40	5.25
		Tuesday	Thursday	Saturday

All trains were timed to connect with those on the N.E.R.

Fares: —

The fares in 1907 were set as follows: —

Pateley Bridge — Wath	SINGLE		RETURN	
	1st	3rd	1st	3rd
Pateley Bridge — Wath	3d.	1½d.	6d.	3d.
Pateley Bridge — Ramsgill	8d.	4d.	1/4d.	8d.
Pateley Bridge — Lofthouse	1/0d.	6d.	2/0d.	1/0d.

By 1927, the third class fares had been altered to: —

Pateley Bridge — Wath	2½d.
Pateley Bridge — Ramsgill	6d.
Pateley Bridge — Lofthouse	9d.

Excursion fares were also available in conjunction with the North Eastern Railway, with the following fares: —

	FIRST	THIRD
Pateley Bridge — Wath	6d.	6d.
Pateley Bridge — Ramsgill	1/0d.	6d.
Pateley Bridge — Lofthouse	1/6d.	9d.

It is worth noting that the North Eastern Railway charged 5% interest on advertising excursions, and for issuing through tickets to the Nidd Valley Light Railway.

In July 1929, the Waterworks Committee recommended that fares be reduced to meet increased competition from local bus services.

From the opening of the line, a rate of 1d. per 1 lb. for any distance was levied for the carriage of newspapers. It was the responsibility of Bradford City Libraries to provide a suitable selection of newspapers for the Reading Room at Scar House site.

Tickets

The ticket system used enabled passengers to break their journey at any point en route.

Signalling

It was originally intended that the railway should be worked by the tablet system, but ordinary signalling was installed, the only signal box on the line being at Pateley Bridge. Each station was connected to the terminus by telephone and each had a lever frame on the platform for working the signals. All the signalling on the line was installed by J.B.Saunders & Co. Ltd.

Buildings

All carriage sheds and goods sheds on the line were built by Humphrey & Co. The four goods sheds were to cost £582, whilst the carriage shed near Pateley Bridge station cost £548. All the stations on the line were generally similar in appearance. This was no doubt done for economic reasons and this was helpful later, for in 1921 plans were considered for adapting Wath and Ramsgill stations for residential purposes at a cost of £100 each. However, little seems to have been done about this matter, for in 1937 similar plans were proposed, this time covering Ramsgill and Lofthouse, and a cost of £300.

OTHER RAILWAYS IN THE NIDD VALLEY

1.   Nidd Valley Branch, North Eastern Railway

This line was important to the Nidd Valley Light Valley as it formed
its connection with the outside world — the line over which materials were
carried to build the line, and over which materials were taken on demolish-
ing it.

The early history of the branch was described in the opening sections
of this story. The first sod was cut in September 1860, and the line was
opened to traffic in under two years, on May 1st, 1862. The line itself was
11½ miles long, single throughout, with stations at Ripley Valley, Hamps-
thwaite, Birstwith, Darley, Dacre and Pateley Bridge. This event was very
important in the development of Nidderdale and a book published in 1906
had this to say of the railway:—

> "The railway has not only proved a great boon to the inhabitants,
> but has opened out the interesting and picturesque spots in the
> dale to visitors, and is at the present time, being extended from
> Pateley Bridge to Lofthouse."

This latter statement was not entirely true, as we have seen, for it was
the Nidd Valley Light Railway that was busy on construction of the exten-
sion up the valley.

The branch had some very quaint locomotives during its operation by
the North Eastern Railway, but it was their whistles which rendered them
unique. It was claimed by one local resident that the whistles could be heard
"half across Yorkshire". Legend has it that the residents of Pateley used to
drink heavily on their visits to Harrogate, and so the following arrangement
was made with the driver. Ten minutes before the train was due to leave
Harrogate, the whistle was blown, and the blood-curdling sound could be
heard right across the town, fetching the Pateley Bridge residents out of the
public houses in time for the train home.

Then came a sudden change for the line, for during the summer of
1923, a petrol-electric railcar was used on the Harrogate to Pateley service,
being one of two experimental vehicles constructed by the North Eastern
Railway in 1903 for light passenger use. However, the heavy gradients on
the line proved too difficult for the car, and it was transferred to a flatter
part of the N.E.R. system, being finally scrapped around 1930.

One cannot help but wonder if the railcar was introduced at this par-
ticular time in order not to be outdone by the N.V.L.R., who had been
operating their service with the ex-Great Western Railway steam railcar
since 1921.

Steam returned, and services continued throughout two decades and more. However, a sad blow came in 1951, when British Railways decided to close the branch to passengers. This was partly caused by the railway over-pricing — the return fare to Harrogate was 3/- compared with only 2/3 on the bus. And so, on March 31st, 1951, local residents gathered at the station to watch the sad sight of the last passenger train leave for Harrogate.

After the closure, a solitary daily goods train made the journey to Pateley Bridge during the week, but this too ended on October 31st, 1964.

However, during the years since 1951, there has been increased commuter traffic from people living in Pateley Bridge who now work in Harrogate, and between 7 a.m. and 8 a.m. four buses leave the town for Harrogate. If British Railways had been less impetuous in closing the line in 1951, they might now have had a substantial share in this traffic.

Despite the obvious value to passengers, freight traffic was also a considerable money-earner for the line, especially in its early days. A siding was laid from Pateley Bridge Station to the Corn Mill by special arrangement with the owner, Mr. John Ingleby, one of the promoters of the line. Also at Pateley, a crane which could lift ten tons was built to deal with the stone traffic, which for a time was one of the mainstays of the line. Similarly, facilities to aid other local industries were introduced, for example, the sidings into the textile mills at Glasshouses.

Alas, these potentialities were not allowed to help the railway to become a profitable service. In Pateley Bridge today, people sadly say:—

"The diesel trains came ten years too late."

2.   Scot Gate Ash Quarry Tramway, Pateley Bridge.

The history of this line has been outlined earlier; it will suffice to mention the salient points here. It was a rope-worked incline, constructed to standard gauge by George Metcalfe, and was in operation from about 1872 to 1892. A new quarry was opened in 1891 at Drayman's Field, further to the east. Much of the earlier workings and most of the tramway were destroyed in severe storms in 1892, and at one time it was feared that as many as 300 of the workers would lose their jobs as a result. However, it was decided to repair the tramway as soon as possible, with George Metcalfe paying half the cost himself. It was out of use by about 1912.

3.   'Horse Levels'

There were many lead mines in the Nidderdale area and, at one time, quite an extensive system of horse-operated narrow gauge railways was used to serve them. These lines were known as 'horse levels' because they were built wide enough to take a horse or pony hauling a train of wagons, and were usually about 6'6" high by 4' wide.

Such a railway seems to have been the Blayshaw Gill Tramway. This was built into the hillside at Blayshaw Gill, near Lofthouse, to extract lead from the limestone and grit. It was laid on a level boring extending ½ mile into the hill and was closed by about 1909. It was the site of the 'Blayshaw Boggle' incident narrated earlier.

Other systems are known to have existed but their exact location is unknown. One other line is certain, that at Harris Shaft, in the the Craven Moor complex of mines, some 3 miles west of Pateley Bridge. A 'tramway' is also marked on plans of the nearby Cockhill Mine.

4. Blayshaw Marble Quarry Railway

The Blayshaw Marble Quarry was leased by Thomas Whitehead, a Harrogate builder, and Alfred Allot, a Sheffield accountant, in the late 1860's. It was their intention to build a railway from the quarry to Pateley Bridge, but no evidence exists that work was ever started on this line. By 1876, Allot was attempting to find someone to take over the lease from him. The quarry was re-opened in 1922 to produce marble for the Ramsgill and Summerbridge War Memorials.

5.   Mention might also be made of two small narrow gauge systems a couple of miles away from Lofthouse, on the other side of the hills, which might be classed as more typical waterworks railways than the N.V.L.R.

One was built by Leeds Corporation Waterworks from Masham Station to the site of a reservoir at Leighton. This was built to 2' gauge and was begun around 1905.

The other line was owned by Harrogate Corporation Waterworks for its reservoir at Roundhill, adjoining Leighton. This was of 1'11½" gauge, and was operated by three saddle tank locomotives named "Harrogate", "Claro" and "Masham". These were sold just before the First World War, and replaced by two paraffin powered Koppel locomotives, which were later scrapped on completion of the project.

BIBLIOGRAPHY

The Nidd Valley Light Railway has been surprisingly little documented; the only concise account of the line that has appeared in book form up to the present time is to be found in H.Hird's 'Bradford in History', pages 178–189, which gives a detailed account of the development of the line.

Other accounts of the railway that have appeared in periodical articles, mostly in the 'Railway Magazine', the following references to which may be helpful:—

Vol.28	1911	p.313–317
Vol.60	1927	p.463–466
Vol.79	1936	p.354/372–373
Vol.81	1937	p.222
Vol.93	1947	p.333
Vol.98	1952	p.143

There is also an article in the Railway & Travel Monthly, Vol.10., April 1915, pages 230–234.

The information in this work has been drawn from many dozens of books on Yorkshire, and on railways in general, and for anyone who is interested in the background history of Nidderdale, I include here some of the works which I have found of great interest:—

Speight. H.   From Nun Monkton to Whernside   1906

Speight. H.   Upper Nidderdale, with the Forest of Knaresborough   1906

Whitehead. T. 'Illustrated Guide to Nidderdale . . .'   1932